Original title:
The Oakwood Chronicles

Copyright © 2025 Creative Arts Management OÜ
All rights reserved.

Author: Samuel Kensington
ISBN HARDBACK: 978-1-80567-442-9
ISBN PAPERBACK: 978-1-80567-741-3

Odyssey of the Oaklands

In the forest where the squirrels jest,
A tree trunk wore a goofy vest.
The raccoons danced a silly jig,
While owls hooted at a dancing pig.

A mushroom tried to start a band,
With beetles clapping on demand.
The sun peeked through the leafy green,
As critters laughed at the silly scene.

The grasshoppers sang a funny song,
While ants marched in, all proud and strong.
The bushes whispered secrets low,
As rabbits hopped in for the show.

The day wrapped up with a laugh so loud,
As the moon chuckled over the crowd.
In oaklands vibrant, a tale was spun,
Where nature's whims brought endless fun.

Experiences Engraved in Shade

Under branches wide and grand,
Lizards sunbathed on warm sand.
A squirrel wore a tiny hat,
And claimed he was the real aristocrat.

Beneath the shade of oaks so stout,
A chipmunk planned a sing-a-out.
With catchy tunes, he stole the scene,
While bees buzzed in a funky routine.

The shadows danced with playful light,
As beetles held a dance-off night.
The frogs croaked laughs in silly tones,
Inventing jokes about garden gnomes.

So here's to days of laughter bright,
In the dappled shade that feels just right.
For every twig that bends and sways,
Holds stories of fun in leafy ways.

The Last Song of the Oak

In the heart of the forest, a croaking frog,
Sings a tune to the curious log.
The squirrels dance, with acorn hats,
While wise old owl just laughs at that.

A raccoon joins in, with a tambourine,
Making music like none you've seen.
When the sun sets low, they start to sway,
To the grand finale of a leafy ballet.

Enigma of the Enchanted Thicket

In a thicket where the bushes blend,
A hedgehog reads, 'Please don't pretend!'
Behind the leaves, the rabbits peek,
The secrets of nature, they softly speak.

The wildflowers giggle, what a sight!
As butterflies argue, who's the best in flight.
But all agree, when the moon is bright,
The love for fun gives the best delight.

Chronicles of Nature's Mystics

The toadstools gather for a grand debate,
About the best method to hibernate.
The bumblebees buzz in harmony,
While fireflies twinkle in jubilee.

Mice fetch cheese from the hedgerow's stash,
Sneaking treats for a midnight bash.
And the old oak chuckles from above,
For in this madness, there's always love.

The Fables Carved in Wood

In tale-telling rings, the beetles spin,
With laughter and stories, let the fun begin!
The woodpecker drums on a hollow tree,
While crickets chirp, 'Come dance with me!'

The tales unfold under starlit skies,
With each fleeting moment, wisdom flies.
The forest's laughter weaves through the night,
As creatures unite in pure delight.

Beneath the Whispering Canopy

In a forest where squirrels play,
Whispers dance on branches sway.
Mice tell tales of cheese so grand,
While owls chuckle, taking a stand.

Frogs croak jokes by the pond's side,
With winks and giggles, they won't hide.
The raccoons plan their heist with flair,
While chipmunks plot, with nuts to share.

Sunlight sparkles through the leaves,
Laughter stirs as it believes.
Beneath the canopy, joys take flight,
In the woods, everything feels just right.

Pinecone Prophecies and Acorn Dreams

Acorns gather for a meet,
Discussing plans for their next feat.
Pinecones roll in with wit so bright,
Promising dreams of a tree-top height.

Squirrels bring maps, all jumbled and torn,
While rabbits hop in, a bit forlorn.
"Let's plant these dreams, see what they grow!"
Together they laugh, putting on a show.

They plot and scheme, a grand design,
With giggles echoing like sweet old wine.
In their muddles, wisdom shines clear,
Even silly plans can bring good cheer.

Secrets of Sylvan Shadows

Beneath the boughs where shadows play,
Lies a party that goes all day.
With critters dancing in silly shoes,
And trees sharing gossip, it's all good news.

Badgers sing songs of yesteryear,
While hedgehogs roll out, spreading cheer.
Fungi glow with a mischievous grin,
Whispering secrets like they've just sinned.

Every rustle and giggle invites,
A fellowship of woodland delights.
In shadows deep, laughter finds its way,
Amidst the chaos, all join the fray.

Mirth of the Mossy Realm

In the mossy realm, where giggles bloom,
Toadstools bounce with the finest tune.
With each plop of mud, there's splashing fun,
As lizards leap beneath the sun.

Jellybeans sprout from mushroom caps,
While crickets share their funny mishaps.
The porcupines wear hats made of leaves,
Being dapper as they play, no one believes.

In this joyous, lively green space,
Each critter's grin finds its own place.
Laughter echoes, nature's sweet herald,
In the mossy realm, all hearts are unfurled.

Echoes of the Woodland Spirits

In the woods where squirrels chatter,
A raccoon wears a hat—what's the matter?
He dances with a chipmunk on a log,
While rabbits are lost in a curious fog.

Wise old owls hoot jokes at night,
Making the fireflies giggle in delight.
Slippery frogs play leapfrog with glee,
While the porcupines poke fun—we're all free!

The Enchanted Grove

In the grove where the fairies hide,
Bumbles the bee gets stuck on a ride.
He buzzes and wiggles, no way to break free,
While the gnomes all chuckle, sipping on tea.

A grumpy old tree complains of the breeze,
Says, "Young saplings dance like they own the trees!"
But the roots all giggle, deep down in their place,
For the leaves know the truth—it's a wild race!

Secrets of the Lost Glade

In the glade where whispers abound,
A lost sock is found, in a roundabout sound.
The mushrooms all giggle, they start a parade,
As hedgehogs applaud with their tiny brigade.

A silly squirrel tells tales of his stash,
While clumsy deer stumble, their legs start to crash.
With snickers and snorts, the woodland unites,
In laughter, they forget all their frights!

Timeworn Tales of the Forest

In forests forgotten where shadows might creep,
A bear tells old stories while the owls all sleep.
He roars in delight, his tales full of cheer,
While rabbits throw popcorn, there's no need to fear.

An ancient old tree holds secrets galore,
But forgets the punchline—oh, what a bore!
As the crow takes a dive, all the critters all crack,
And the forest erupts with a joyful clack!

Where the Wild Ferns Dance

In the glade where ferns sway,
A squirrel tells jokes all day.
With acorns they laugh and tease,
Wobbling lightly in the breeze.

Beneath the shade of leafy hats,
A family of cheerful spats.
The rabbits hop and play charades,
While hedgehogs laugh at silly parades.

When sun sets, they share sweet pie,
Singing songs that make foxes cry.
Dancing shadows, moonlight prance,
In this lively, leafy dance.

So if you wander in the wood,
Join the fun, it's really good.
With every wiggle, jump, and skip,
You'll find the joy in nature's trip.

Lanterns of Dusk and Dawn

When night falls, the fireflies glow,
They flicker like stars dancing low.
Crickets chirp their evening tune,
While owls howl at the silly moon.

In the morning, the sunbeams play,
Chasing sleepy shadows away.
Woodpeckers tap a jolly beat,
While deer join in with tiny feet.

The squirrels start their coffee shop,
With acorn lattes, they won't stop.
And all the trees join in the fun,
As laughter sparkles, one by one.

So hang your worries, let them douse,
In this woodland of magic, I espouse.
For every dawn and dusk we meet,
There's joy in every little beat.

Guardians of the Timbered Path

Beneath the boughs, where secrets hum,
A band of critters starts to drum.
With leaves for shields and sticks like swords,
They fight for snacks and pickled gourds.

Badger leads with a mighty cheer,
As all the woodland friends draw near.
They plan a heist on farmer's stash,
A quest for carrots in a flash!

With toadstools as their solid bases,
They plot their sneak and merry chases.
But laughter echoes, plans go wild,
For every proud knight's a playful child.

In the end, it's just good fun,
At day's end, they share what's won.
Guardians of the path so grand,
With hearts of laughter, united stand.

Reveries in the Forest's Embrace

In the forest's hold so tight,
Bears discuss their latest fright.
A picnic gone wrong, oh dear me,
Honey mixed up with a sea of tea.

Near the brook, ants hold a feast,
With crumbs that make them say the least.
They giggle and dance in silly rows,
As worms join in with wiggly bows.

Mushrooms wear hats, oh what a sight,
As fireflies twinkle in delight.
They share their tales of mishaps grand,
While bushes chuckle, hand in hand.

So if you hear the laughter soar,
Join the revelry and explore.
In this realm where whimsy's a place,
Find joyous moments, full of grace.

The Foliage Whispers Back

In the woods where squirrels chatter,
Leaves gossip like friends in a clatter.
A raccoon in a hat waves hello,
While blue jays strut with a grand show.

Branches sway with a playful tease,
Escaping the weight of the buzzing bees.
A chipmunk's dance steals the spotlight,
While the wise old owl tries not to giggle tonight.

Mushrooms gather for tea and chit-chat,
Complaining about the cheeky brat.
The shadows laugh, oh what a spree,
In this forest, joy runs free!

When leaves tickle and shake with delight,
Nature's comedy is the true highlight.
Join the fun in this leafy place,
Where even the trees have a silly face.

Nature's Memoir in Botanic Lines

A daffodil sneezes with flair,
And the daisies giggle without a care.
A fern flips its fronds just to tease,
While cacti dance with such great ease.

In the meadow, butterflies slip and slide,
While dandelions boast their fluffy pride.
Forgetful ants march in a parade,
Chasing crumbs in a messy cascade.

Clouds above do a cotton candy swirl,
As wind plays tricks on the leaves with a twirl.
Nature's tales are funny, it's true,
A leafy sitcom for me and you!

Frogs croak jokes in a slick manner,
While rabbits join in with a spiffy planner.
This memoir of greenery is quite the jest,
With nature's humor, we're truly blessed.

In the Arms of the Ancient Trees

Beneath the boughs, shadows play tricks,
While squirrels make plans with their secret flicks.
The trunks are wise, with stories to tell,
Of a woodpecker's tap and a rabbit's rebel spell.

Branches huddle like gossipy friends,
Sharing wild tales that never quite end.
A woodchuck smirks, it's up to no good,
Pulling pranks like a mischievous brood.

Dancing leaves catch the sun's golden gleam,
While roots underground plot a strange dream.
"Who's the tallest?" they argue with glee,
As shadows chuckle, "Not quite, you see!"

In these ancient arms, we find such delight,
With all the creatures playing all night.
Nature's embrace is packed with gags,
In this leafy playground, laughter swag.

The Allure of the Verdant Veil

A curtain of leaves lets secrets fly,
As butterflies gossip and giggles sigh.
Mossy carpets offer a soft bed,
While ladybugs tickle, 'til you see red.

Vines twist and tangle in a playful race,
As frogs leap forth with a splash and a grace.
A nest of sparrows sings out a tune,
While dandelions dance beneath the moon.

In the underbrush, a party ensues,
With mushrooms and bugs sharing their views.
The woodland charm pulls fun from the air,
In this verdant veil, we all share a dare!

Laugh with the petals, unwind with the bark,
In this lush green world, there's always a spark.
Nature's allure is funny, indeed,
Join in the frolic, and you'll feel freed.

Shadows Cast by Twilight Leaves

In the dusk of pines, squirrels play,
Chasing shadows, come what may.
A raccoon wears a hat too big,
While a rabbit pulls a little jig.

Owls hoot out a silly rhyme,
As fireflies dance, not keeping time.
A fox sneezes from the dust,
And laughs so hard, he bursts with lust.

The clouds parade with silly grins,
As beetles plot their tiny sins.
A moose slipped in a muddy pool,
He splashed his friends; now who's the fool?

In the twilight glow, the antics weave,
Nature's comedy, hard to believe.
Leaves chuckle softly in the breeze,
While chipmunks plan their next big tease.

Songs of the Forest's Soul

The trees are singing, but with a twist,
Each note a giggle, you get the gist.
A woodpecker's beat is pure delight,
As he taps away, with all his might.

The brook hums tunes that bubble and flow,
While frogs croak out in a musical show.
A turtle struts, all slow and grand,
Pretending to lead, with a wave of a hand.

Chipmunk choirs gather for a show,
Each one puffed up, putting on a glow.
A deer joins in with a prance and a leap,
While the sun laughs, as it starts to sleep.

In this concert of nature's charm,
Even the trees can't hide their warm,
As the night descends, they still convey,
A playful tune that just won't sway.

Echoing Footfalls on Forest Floors

Footfalls crunch on leaves and grass,
Each sound a secret, none can surpass.
A bear stumbles with an awkward grace,
Makes all the critters laugh in this place.

A hare hops with a cheeky flair,
While the ants march up without a care.
A cat's paw slips on a muddy patch,
She blinks, surprised—a funny catch!

The sound of laughter fills the air,
As each creature shares a funny scare.
A misstep here, a slip or two,
In the heart of the woods, it's always true.

With echoes bright and spirits high,
The forest bustles beneath the sky.
Each footfall's a story, a giggle galore,
Every step brings us back for more.

The Arbor's Silent Watch

The trees stand tall, yet they have quirks,
With branches dancing as nature smirks.
The bark's got jokes, the leaves just sigh,
  Watching the antics of critters nearby.

A turtle takes a gamble, slow and bold,
  Crossing paths that never get old.
  A wise old owl attempts a wink,
But a squirrel steals his glasses—what do you think?

A badger shares a snack with a crow,
They argue over seeds, then laugh as they go.
  The sun sets low with a golden hue,
  Painting the mishaps of everyone too.

In the quiet, the trees have tales,
Of giggling raccoons and clumsy snails.
They witness life, both wild and sweet,
With every lost step, life's bittersweet.

Threads of Life Among the Trees

In the shade where squirrels prance,
My coffee spills, oh what a chance!
A birdsong rings, a silly cheer,
As acorns drop from high, oh dear!

The branches wave, they seem to jest,
"Your hat is on the ground, you pest!"
Beneath the leaves, a rabbit chuckles,
As I chase him, tripping over chuckles!

The woodpecker taps a cheeky beat,
While I dance in my two left feet.
The trees can't help but share a grin,
As I take another tumble, spin!

Nature's wits keep me in line,
With every laugh, the sun will shine.
In this place of silly cheer,
Life's a jest; come laugh with me here!

The Soliloquy of Silent Woods

In whispers soft, the branches sigh,
"Is that a raccoon or just a pie?"
I pause to think, then burst with glee,
As mossy shoes engulf my feet.

A critter schemes in leafy shade,
Plotting pranks, a grand charade.
The trees declare a royal court,
With bark-judges for their squabbling sport!

An oak quips, "That's quite a hat!"
While the willows cheer, "Look at that!"
The forest floor comes alive with jest,
As I act the fool, I'm truly blessed!

Each leaf is laughter, sweet and wild,
In my heart, the woods are my child.
Embrace the light, let worries flee,
In this realm of jest, we will always be.

Chronicles of the Twisted Timber

A crooked tree with a laugh so grand,
Tells tales of squirrels, a nutty band.
"Yesterday, I saw them race,
One slipped and fell, oh what a face!"

The branches twist with secrets bold,
While mushrooms giggle, stories told.
A snail declares, "I'll win this game!"
While I just sit, a tad bit lame.

The thickets bloom with chirpy glee,
As moss nudges me, "You can't flee!"
The roots entwined in silly prance,
In this wood, we're all in a dance.

So gather 'round the twisted trunks,
With every laugh, we shake off funks.
In the forest's heart, we find our flair,
Chronicles of fun float in the air!

The Elders in the Enclosed Grove

In an old grove where secrets dwell,
The elders chuckle, weaving tales so well.
"Remember when we danced in rain?"
"Ah yes, you slipped, you felt quite pain!"

With bark that's faded, wisdom flows,
They laugh at each other's creaky prose.
"Trees grow old, but jokes stay young,
Just take a look at that silly sprung!"

A ladybug sings, joining the jest,
While owls dub the night a festive fest.
Time is a comedy, laughter our thread,
In this cozy grove, where we rarely dread.

So let's toast to years of silly cheer,
Among the elders, I shed my fear.
In every knot, there's a story crafted,
In the enclosed grove, joy's never shafted!

Chronicles by the Water's Edge

Once a frog fancied a boat,
'Twas really just a leaf afloat.
He pushed and paddled with flair,
But ended up tangled in despair.

Fish laughed, splashing with glee,
While frogs quarreled, as frogs do, you see.
The water rippled with jesting cheer,
As every misstep rang loud and clear.

A turtle cheered, 'What a silly mess!'
But the frog just flexed, wearing his best.
He claimed it was all in great fun,
And vowed to be number one!

So next time you see a frog in a rowboat,
Remember the tale of that leaf-turned-float.
Laughter is what life's all about,
Even if sometimes you're filled with doubt.

Petals and Pulp

A flower grew in a paper mill,
With petals made of every skill.
She danced and swayed at the daily grind,
While paper mates were far less kind.

'Oh, look at her,' they all did chat,
'Flaunting colors; the nerve and the spat!'
But the flower just took it in stride,
Swayed her petals with a goofy pride.

Then one day, a bee flew by,
Said, 'Your style makes paper fly!'
The other blooms looked quite astounded,
While the flower giggled, joy abounded.

In the end, it was quite surreal,
A flower with confidence, oh what a deal!
In the world of pulp, she found her slot,
With laughter and petals, she changed the plot.

a Fable Unfurled

In a clearing, there lived a wise old sage,
Who declared, 'Let's turn a new page!'
He gathered the critters for a grand show,
But forgot how to start; oh, what a blow!

The rabbit hopped, ate some grass,
While the tortoise said, 'Move your... fast!'
Birds squawked loud in confused delight,
As the wise old sage scratched his head in fright.

Finally, he spoke with a booming cheer,
'Let's tell a tale, gather near!'
But the only tale was about lunch,
So everyone scrambled, a hungry bunch.

Now when you hear a fable unfold,
Remember the sage, nervous and bold.
With laughter and folly, tales often grow,
A story that's funny is a story we know!

Shadows of Growth Amidst Grassy Depths

Beneath the grass, plants plotted a play,
'Let's start a troupe, hip-hip-hooray!'
So roots wiggled and leaves took flight,
In hopes of a performance that felt just right.

A gopher rose with a heartfelt song,
His singing was off-key, but never wrong.
The daisies joined with a hop and sway,
While the ferns sighed, 'Oh dear, come what may!'

The show began at the crack of dawn,
But a squirrel dashed through, and then it was gone!
With nuts flying high, chaos ensued,
And all the plants burst out laughing, good mood renewed.

So if you stroll through the grassy loops,
Listen closely for planty whoops,
For laughter it seems, is a mighty tool,
Even if the performers don't follow the rule!

The Grove's Hidden Narrative

In the grove, secrets were ripe,
Of trees who thought they could type.
They gathered round, with branches so spry,
Scribbling stories that made squirrels cry.

One tree wrote of love, oh so sweet,
While another claimed, 'I've invented the beat!'
Acorns rolled with a thundering cheer,
As branches clapped and whispered near.

But when the winds blew with a sigh,
Not one could find the paper they'd try.
Leaves fell in laughter, doodles in the air,
For tales were best when shared with flair.

Thus, in groves where stories are grown,
Remember, fun often takes the throne.
For narratives told with giggles and grins,
Make every tale a merry spin!

The Wisdom of the Oldest Tree

In the forest lived a sage,
With leaves of green, he took center stage.
He chuckled loud, with branches wide,
Tales of squirrels, his trusted guide.

Why do birds wear their feathers bright?
To impress the clouds, with all their might!
The acorns giggle, they fall with flair,
They land on heads, oh, what a dare!

He barked wise words, like a funky beat,
Telling mushrooms how to dance on their feet.
"Tickle the wind! Give it a whirl!"
All in the woods, laughed with a twirl.

A critter once asked, with a curious stare,
"Old Tree, what's the secret? You seem so rare!"
"Keep your roots deep, laugh every day,
And wear your age like a crown, come what may!"

Costumes of Earth and Sky

Dressed in greens, the grasses sway,
While daisies twirl in a bright ballet.
Clouds wear gowns, so light and puffy,
Nature's prom is absolutely fluffy!

Rocks don capes of mossy green,
While raindrops sparkle like a scene.
The wind's the DJ, spinning tunes,
While critters dance beneath the moons.

"Who wore it best?" a beetle questioned,
In vibrant hues, his shell must've mentioned.
The sun chuckled, with rays so bright,
"Wear what you love, fashion's delight!"

As owls sport glasses on wise old faces,
And fireflies light up in glowing graces.
The forest cheers in a whimsical show,
With nature's costumes putting on a glow!

Whispers Among Ancient Trees

Old trunks chat in hushed delight,
Swapping secrets, day and night.
"What's that racket? Oh, just a deer,
He's trying to dance, we can barely hear!"

Squirrels gossip from treetop high,
"Did you see that? He tried to fly!"
Barking laughter, branches creak,
Nature's humor is far from bleak.

With a rustle, a wise owl spoke,
"I overheard a tree just choke!"
"Why so serious?" a young one asked,
When laughter is all, we should be basked.

As breezes tickle the leaves up high,
Echoes of laughter fill the sky.
In the heart of woods, joy is found,
Among ancient trees where fun abounds!

Shadows Beneath the Canopy

Under the shade, where giggles grow,
Frogs tell jokes, putting on a show.
With shadows dancing, a mischievous game,
Laughter rings out, never the same.

"Knock, knock," the old tree called out,
"Who's there?" the bushes began to shout.
"Leaf." "Leaf who?" "Leaf it to me,
I'll keep it shady and care-free!"

Beneath the boughs, stories trope,
Where stories spin and laughter's rope.
With frogs in tuxedos, they all cheer,
In the glades, the fun draws near!

So join the fun in the moon's sweet glow,
Where shadows answer, and laughter flows.
The forest a stage, nature's bright spree,
Whispers of joy, all wild and free!

Rustling Tales of the Greenwood

In the glen where squirrels play,
Nuts are stashed, come what may.
A rabbit slips on a banana peel,
And lands right near a dancing eel.

The hedgehog wears a tiny hat,
As a wise old owl says, "What's that?"
They giggle loud at raccoons' pranks,
In these woods, they give their thanks.

The trees all whisper with delight,
As foxes plan a starry night.
With fireflies dancing in a show,
They toast to friends they love and know.

So join the fun, don't skip a beat,
In this place where critters meet.
Where every rustle tells a tale,
Come on down, don't let it fail!

The Heartbeat of Twisted Roots

Down by the creek, a frog named Lou,
Tried to sing but forgot the tune.
A fish jumped out and waved a fin,
Said, "Just relax, let the fun begin!"

The twisted roots have stories bold,
Of silly gnomes and treasure old.
A fairy lost her sparkly shoe,
While beetles formed a marching crew.

Beneath the boughs, a picnic's spread,
Gather 'round, remember, it's said:
Cheese is great, but laughs are better,
Just keep an eye on that flighty sweater!

A dance-off starts, oh what a sight,
With squirrels spinning in sheer delight.
The twigs snap to the rhythm's beat,
In twisted roots, the heart's a treat!

Chronicles of the Whispering Pines

In pines that whisper tales of yore,
A raccoon grins and asks for more.
A game of hide-and-seek is on,
With giggles echoing till the dawn.

A hedgehog tried to fit in a pot,
Only to learn, that's just not hot!
The pinecones laugh as they fall down,
While bushes conspire to share their crown.

The breezy sounds; they make a tune,
With fireflies dancing under the moon.
A sleepy turtle hums away,
Making dreams of nuts and hay.

When morning comes, the stage is set,
For furry acts we won't forget.
In whispering pines, where tales revive,
Everyone's welcome; all are alive!

Sylvan Journeys and Lost Legends

Through the leaves where shadows play,
A fox is lost, or so they'd say.
A map made of crumbs leads the way,
To a bakery, bright as day!

Wandering owls with oversized hats,
Debate the merits of squeaky bats.
A squirrel juggles acorns with flair,
While prancing deer stop to stare.

In the glades, where stories bloom,
They're charting paths to a snacky room.
Laughs are shared with every turn,
In the woods, the heart does burn.

So if you wander and find delight,
Join in the fun, from day to night.
For in these journeys, the legend's clear,
Laughter's the treasure that brings us near!

The Forest's Heartbeat

In the grove where squirrels dance,
A raccoon wears a silly pants.
Trees whisper secrets to the breeze,
While bees buzz tunes with utmost ease.

Leaves perform a jolly jig,
The pond's a stage for a plump big pig.
Frogs croak out a quirky song,
Come join the fun, it won't be long!

Sunlight twinkles through the boughs,
Nature's stage, and we are cows.
Hilarity grows like ivy wide,
In this wood, where joy can't hide.

So if you hear a laugh nearby,
A lumberjack's playing with a pie.
The trees all grin, it's clear to see,
This forest thrives on lunacy!

A Symphony of Wood and Wind

The wind plays tunes through branches high,
While owls ask questions, oh my, oh my!
Woodpeckers tap on trunks with glee,
Creating beats for you and me.

A rabbit hops, a dance so fine,
Wearing a hat, he's sipping wine.
The hedgehogs roll in a comic spree,
While turtles argue who's fastest, whee!

Under the boughs where giggles thrive,
Grasshoppers compete, oh what a jive!
The trees sway to the rhythm sweet,
Join in the fun, get up on your feet!

As night descends, the critters cheer,
A shadow puppet show appears!
With laughter echoing through the land,
This woodwind symphony is oh so grand!

The Chronicles of the Elderwood

In Elderwood where stories bloom,
There lives a cat who sweeps the room.
With whiskers long and hat askew,
His tales of mischief are all too true.

A fox reads tales to the weary moon,
While mice throw acorns to the tune.
With every word, the shadows dance,
A comedy that'll make you prance.

Squirrels climb trees and shout out loud,
As if they're surfing on a cloud.
With each crackle of the leaf below,
The elder trees laugh in a row.

So gather close around the fire,
And listen to tales that never tire.
In Elderwood, the fun's a flight,
Each night's a story, each laugh's a light!

Amidst the Canopies of Time

Among the branches, time stands still,
With birds who joke and never chill.
The bumblebees compete in style,
As giggles echo for a mile.

An old oak tree, wise and spry,
Tells tales of squirrels who dare to fly.
With every rustle, a new delight,
As shadows twist in soft moonlight.

The brook sings ballads with a splash,
While rabbits duke it out for cash.
The trees all chuckle as they sway,
At all the antics of the day.

So tread with care in time's embrace,
For in this wood, you'll find your place.
Amongst the canopies, laughter chimes,
As every creature breaks the binds.

Whispers of the Ancient Grove

In the grove where secrets dwell,
A squirrel spins a yarn to tell.
It claims the acorns hold a dance,
And every nut has had its chance.

A rabbit laughs, he shakes his tail,
Says he can hop without a fail.
But when he jumps, he trips on roots,
And laughs again in silly hoots.

The owls watch with knowing eyes,
As all the creatures prance and rise.
With every chuckle in the air,
The ancient trees join in the flair.

So wander through this joyful place,
Where every critter finds their space.
With laughter shared among the boughs,
Nature's fun, alive, it sows.

Echoes Beneath the Boughs

Beneath the boughs, a frog does croak,
He thinks he's wise, that silly bloke.
He tells the bugs to heed his call,
But all they do is laugh and crawl.

A fox, with whiskers oh so grand,
Pretends to lead, yet takes a stand.
He prances like he's king of all,
Until he trips and makes a fall.

The deer giggles, flicks her ear,
At every flaw, she holds them dear.
In echoes loud, the laughter rings,
The forest feels like it's on springs.

So stay awhile beneath these trees,
Where jokes are shared upon the breeze.
With every cheer, life takes its course,
In this wild, enchanted force.

Tales from the Woodland Shadows

In shadows deep, where stories brew,
A hedgehog claims he builds a zoo.
Yet all his beasts are quite unreal,
Just thorns and leaves – what a great deal!

An ant tells tales of grand parades,
Where every crumb is music played.
But when the feast begins to start,
He never gets the tiniest part.

The bees buzz tales of nectar sweet,
Filling their hives with dancing feet.
But when they're caught in sticky woes,
They fashion hats from petals' throes.

So gather round, let laughter grow,
Where woodland shadows freely flow.
In this embrace of jest and cheer,
The forest sings, "Come laugh right here!"

Secrets of the Leafy Canopy

Upon the canopy up high,
A parrot jokes as the sun sweeps by.
He shadows squirrels, mocks their games,
While teasing them with silly names.

The raccoon, known as trickster king,
Sneaks off with snacks and starts to sing.
He claims his stash is full of gold,
But only found old socks – behold!

The trees, they sway and shuffle leaves,
As whispers float on warm evening eves.
With witty puns and laughter pure,
The leafy crown, it does allure.

So leap with joy among the trees,
Where secrets reign and joy's a breeze.
In playful jest, we find our place,
In nature's hug, a warm embrace.

Twilight in the Timberland

As shadows creep in twilight glow,
The squirrels play a game of throw.
They toss acorns, oh what a sight,
While owls hoot, it's quite the night.

The rabbits cheer from their leafy beds,
While ladybugs count, one through tens.
A raccoon sneaks, with mischief in paws,
He steals a snack, and then he withdraws.

The crickets chirp their evening tune,
The fireflies twinkle, a tiny boon.
All creatures dance, as if on cue,
In this forest, always something new!

So gather 'round, don't slip or trip,
Join the fun, take a playful dip.
Under the stars, life feels so grand,
In this whimsical, wooded land.

Nature's Scribe: The Oak's Memoir

An oak with tales, both old and wise,
Whispers secrets under the skies.
A breeze flows through, a gentle nudge,
As the leaves giggle, starting to budge.

Each squirrel scurries, a story to tell,
Of acorn hunts and how they fell.
With branches, they launch a paper plane,
Wishing on winds, ignoring the rain.

The bumblebees buzz in chaotic glee,
While turtles ponder their legacy.
They chat about life, both slow and fast,
In their world, every moment's a blast.

The moonlight glimmers, a silver quill,
The forest scribes tales with a thrill.
With laughter ringing, hearts feel free,
In nature's book, there's comedy.

The Dance of the Swaying Branches

Branches sway with a rhythmic grace,
Like they're competing in a dance space.
The leaves applaud with a rustle and cheer,
As the wind leads them, they have no fear.

A woodpecker taps, joins in the beat,
While chipmunks groove, with rapid feet.
Together they whirl, a merry crew,
Where every step is a moment anew.

The shadows giggle, the light beams grin,
As every sway is a subtle spin.
Beneath the trunks, a laugh echoes bright,
In this dance, everything feels just right.

So take a step, don't just observe,
Join the branches in the sway and curve.
For in this forest, joy intertwines,
A dance of nature, where laughter shines.

Fauna's Folklore and Flora's Fables

In the heart of the woods, stories intertwine,
With fauna's giggles and flora's design.
A fox tells tales of days gone past,
While flowers listen, their colors vast.

A deer prances, adding to the lore,
With every leap, there's something more.
The daisies chuckle at her swift flight,
Whispering secrets in pure delight.

Mice debate the cheese's supremacy,
As ferns sway, granting some clarity.
They giggle and wiggle, sharing their dreams,
In this wild world, nothing's as it seems.

So gather near, for stories unfold,
With laughter like treasures, waiting to be told.
In the company of creatures, big and small,
Each fable's a gift, cherished by all.

Where Roots Whisper Ancient Lore

In the woods where shadows play,
Roots gossip in their funny way.
Trees chuckle, leaves flap in glee,
Squirrels dance, as wild as can be.

A woodpecker taps to join the fun,
While mushrooms giggle, one by one.
The old oak winks with a knotted grin,
Whispering tales of the history within.

A raccoon tumbles, slips on a log,
While frogs croak jokes like an old blog.
The breeze carries laughter near and far,
In this quirky, leafy memoir.

So come to this woodland mischief feast,
Where every creature's a jester at least.
Roots revel in stories, both silly and wise,
In a realm where laughter never dies.

Celestial Reflections in a Serene Glade

In a glade where stars flicker bright,
The moon pulls pranks, what a sight!
Crickets chirp a midnight tune,
While owls wink like a sly cartoon.

The pond mirrors a twinkling sky,
Frogs leap, shrugging, 'Oh, why not try?'
Fireflies flicker, buzzing their lights,
Playing tag through vanishing nights.

A raccoon with a hat tips it low,
He's the dancer while squirrels throw a show.
Leaves shower laughter, like glitter from dreams,
In this magical woodland of bursting seams.

So wander beneath the starry dome,
Where woodland creatures call nature home.
Join the fun, in this playful space,
Where celestial giggles weave magic in place.

A Tapestry of Twisting Roots

Among the roots, a tale unfolds,
In knots and curls, laughter molds.
A hedgehog stands, too proud to roll,
While rabbits hop, with snacks to stole.

Twisting tales, like the roots below,
Snails race slowly, stealing the show.
A wise old tree yawns, stretching wide,
Chuckling at squirrels who comically slide.

The wise tortoise grins at the fuss,
While ants form lines in joyous bus.
Acorns drop like laughs from above,
Creating a patchwork of woodland love.

So come weave through roots, take a chance,
Join in the woods for a merry dance.
In the tapestry spun from earth and cheer,
Every twist a giggle, every curve sincere.

The Woodland Symphony

In the heart of the grove, music swells,
As trees hum tunes, and nature dwells.
A trumpet of birds, a drum of the stream,
Compose the melody, a woodland dream.

Beetles dance like tiny rock stars,
While a pair of foxes strum banjo guitars.
A butterfly swings, gracefully high,
Creating a ballet beneath the blue sky.

The wind whispers softly, the leaves cheer and clap,
A concert of critters; come take a nap!
A tune for the ages, a humorous mix,
In the woodlands where laughter just clicks.

So join the symphony, oh dear friend,
Where nature and mischief happily blend.
In this melodic forest, with every sound,
Life's a funny tune, forever unbound.

Twilight Secrets of the Bark and Moss

In twilight's glow, the squirrels meet,
They share their tales of stolen seeds.
A raccoon plots a snack delight,
Oh, woodland dreams beneath the lights.

The owl hoots loud, a hoot so proud,
But stumbles on a branch, how loud!
The fireflies giggle and buzz around,
While crickets play their nightly sound.

A hedgehog trips upon a root,
Declaring loudly, "What a hoot!"
The trees are laughing with the breeze,
As night unfolds with silly tease.

Bark whispers secrets to the moss,
"Who's the clumsiest?" it's a toss!
Under the stars, with jest and cheer,
Nature's joy, we hold it dear.

Breath of the Earth and Sky

The earth exhales a funny sound,
As worms wiggle in the ground.
The breezes carry jokes so light,
With giggles swirling through the night.

A cloud floats by, a fluffy prank,
Drops a sprinkle, splashes rank.
The daisies dance in bright delight,
Tickling toes with pure sunlight.

A dragonfly swings to and fro,
Chasing shadows, what a show!
Leaves rustle loud, they seem to say,
"Tickle your friend in a leafy way!"

The sky winks down, a mischievous view,
While stars throw sparkles, just for you.
With laughter echoing near and far,
Earth and sky, a playful star.

Reflections in the Forest Stream

In a stream where whispers play,
Fish tell tales in a shiny way.
A frog leaps high, and skips a beat,
Lands with a splash, oh what a feat!

The otters slide on muddy banks,
While turtles strike the silliest pranks.
Reflections giggle with glee and charm,
The forest hums with a happy balm.

Butterflies flit, in colors bright,
Playing tag with the sun's warm light.
A squirrel slips on a shiny stone,
With laughter ringing, he's not alone.

As evening falls, the moon will beam,
Painting silver on the stream.
Every ripple tells a joke,
Nature laughs, it's quite bespoke.

A Tapestry Woven by Wind

The wind weaves through the tall, tall trees,
Sending messages with playful ease.
A branch sways low, a branch sways high,
A dancing tune beneath the sky.

Leaves flutter down in a merry race,
Tickled by breezes, they find their place.
A whistling laugh from a passing bird,
"Catch me if you can!" is what I heard.

The daisies bow with a gentle spin,
As gusts of joy rush in to win.
Through every nook, laughs echo sweet,
An endless melody of happy beats.

In gusts and breezes, the whispers thrive,
Nature's jokes keep the forest alive.
A tapestry spun in nature's embrace,
Where laughter thrives, and joys interlace.

The Requiem of Rustling Leaves

In a glade where squirrels dance,
A chipmunk dared to take a chance.
He stole a nut, so very bold,
Then tripped and tumbled, oh so cold.

The trees, they giggled, leaves gave cheer,
As woodland critters gathered near.
"It's a feast!" the badger cried,
While raccoons rolled from side to side.

A fox, with flair, performed his trick,
He juggled acorns, quick and slick.
Then with a bow, he took a break,
And laughed so hard, he caused a quake.

Amidst the mirth, the owl would coo,
"This forest life, what fun to view!"
Yet still they fret, the woods so wide,
With silly fables, they confide.

Legacies of the Lush Land

In wild woods where laughter thrives,
The critters talk and share their lives.
The raccoon boasts of midnight raids,
While blue jays gossip in the glades.

A turtle's tale of speed and grace,
Had everyone rolling, a slowpoke race.
"I'll teach you all!" the rabbit said,
But fell down laughing, 'till he bled.

The bees wore hats, mustaches too,
Buzzing about like they were new.
"We're the kings of sweet delight!"
They danced and spun, what a sight!

Legacies told in puns and quips,
Of forest friends and silly trips.
For in this land, both lush and grand,
Each laugh's a treasure, close at hand.

Beneath the Boughs

Beneath the boughs, a party's set,
With snacks of berries, no room to fret.
A hedgehog tries to play charades,
But rolls into the berry glades.

A parrot squawks, a stand-up set,
His punchlines hit—oh what a vet!
The rabbits chuckle, holding paws,
While in the back, the badger snores.

Each tale unfolds with doodles drawn,
Of fairies giggling until dawn.
The fireflies join, with lights aglow,
As mischief sparks them to and fro.

In laughter echoing through the trees,
Silly shadows dance with ease.
For every critter knows the truth,
Beneath the boughs, we find our youth.

Dreams Unfold

In dreamy woods where wishes play,
A squirrel dreams of nuts today.
He leaps and bounds, but oh dear me,
He dives headfirst into a tree!

A raccoon winks, plans on a heist,
But ends up snagged, 'twas not so nice.
With sticky paws, he can't retreat,
His snack now done, what a defeat!

The wise old owl spins bedtime tales,
Of dance parades and feathered sails.
With every hoot, laughter's spread,
While daydreams swirl around their heads.

From boughs above to roots below,
Life's little bloopers steal the show.
In forests deep, where giggles stay,
Dreams unfold in the funniest way.

The Yearning Winds of the Forest

Winds confess what trees have shared,
Of rambunctious friends who've dared.
A chipmunk sprinted, wild with glee,
But lost his hat—oh, what a spree!

The winds, they chuckle, swirling round,
Stirring leaves up from the ground.
A turtle sighs, "Oh stop this breeze!"
As leaves dance madly, mocking heaves.

With stories fresh, the forest sings,
Of wacky squabbles and silly flings.
Each gust a laugh, each breeze a jest,
In crazy winds, they find their best.

So let the winds keep secrets bright,
Of woodland antics, pure delight.
For here in nature, fun takes flight,
As laughter carries through the night.

When Cedar Meets Sky

When a cedar met the sky, oh what a chat,
It spoke of clouds, while wearing a hat.
The clouds just giggled, they swirled around,
Till a squirrel yelled, 'Shift, we're losing ground!'

The cedar sighed, 'I wish I could fly!'
The sky just laughed, 'Well, you're way too spry!'
So they danced together, in a leafy jig,
While birds were laughing at the sight so big.

Chronicles from the Forest Floor

Down on the forest floor, where mushrooms play,
Fungi gossip at the end of the day.
A beetle pranced, all shiny and spry,
Said, 'I'm the king!' to a passing fly.

A twig snapped loud, a rabbit took flight,
Screaming, 'I'm late for the vegetable night!'
The chorus of crickets burst into cheer,
While a turtle grumbled, 'I'll be there next year!'

Legends of the Leafy Keep

In the Leafy Keep, legends grow tall,
Where acorns debated, who's the king of them all?
One said, 'It's me, I'll sprout into a tree!'
Another just chuckled, 'You're just a wee pea!'

Mice held a council, they squeaked and they squealed,
Over who's the fleetest, who'd never yield.
An owl, perched high, said with a hoot,
'You're all quite the jesters, adorned in your loot!'

The Oak's Embrace

In the shade of an oak, two friends did lay,
One said, 'Is that breeze coming to play?'
The other replied, with a chuckle so light,
'It's just the oak dancing in the night!'

A raccoon peered out, all curious and sly,
'Are you both nuts or just passing by?'
They giggled and tossed acorns to the ground,
'In the oak's embrace, joy is always found!'

Glories of the Greenwood

In the woods where squirrels play,
Acorns fall like rain each day.
Barking dogs and laughing trees,
Nature's jokes bring everyone to tease.

Rabbits hop in silly lines,
Chasing tails and giggling shrines.
Mushrooms dance in dappled light,
While owls hoot with all their might.

Branches wave like old, wise friends,
With whispered tales that never ends.
Dancing leaves in breezy raves,
Call the critters, "Come, be brave!"

So grab your hats and join the spree,
In laughing woods where you'll be free.
Join the fun, don't miss the cue,
The greenwood calls—it's all for you!

The Arboreal Chronicles

Once a tree with branches wide,
Had a bird who often cried.
"Why don't you sing a happy tune?"
The bark replied, "I leave that to the moon!"

In the forest, fungi dreams,
Playful shadows, glittering beams.
A wise old owl wearing specs,
Watched the critters making wrecks.

Bouncing bumblebees in a mess,
Wore tiny hats—they looked so fresh!
"Bees in hats!" the rabbit cried,
As wise old owl just laughed and sighed.

With tales of trees that dance and sway,
Their fun-filled lives make bright the day.
Join the joy, no need to pine,
In this arboreal world so fine!

Ethereal Echoes in the Evergreen

In the evergreen, the whispers flow,
Tall tales told by trees that glow.
Bushy shrubs and secrets wide,
Echo laughter where fairies hide.

Chipmunks wear their winter vests,
Strutting like they're kinder guests.
With a twirl, they start to dance,
As nature plays a merry romance.

Hearts of pine and needles bright,
Flicker gently in the night.
Mystic glows and shadows jump,
Join the fun and skip the grump!

So waddle on, you silly one,
In evergreen where joy's begun.
Silly echoes make us cheer,
In this enchanted wood, my dear!

The Canopy's Cradle

In a cradle made of leaves,
Lies a nest of laughing thieves.
Raccoons play with shiny things,
Underneath the choir that sings.

Caterpillars in a line,
Swaying in time, feeling fine.
With a twist, they become a show,
Just to see who'll steal the glow!

Whiskers twitch and tails do flip,
As the grasshoppers take a trip.
Launching high and landing low,
The canopy hosts a funny show!

So dance beneath the glowing skies,
With laughter bright and joyful sighs.
In the cradle where all can play,
Every moment's a holiday!

The Dusty Trails beneath Old Boughs

In the woods where squirrels play,
A raccoon wears a hat today.
He struts around with such a flair,
The other critters stop and stare.

A rabbit hops, he's late for tea,
While ants parade, so proud and free.
A fox rolls in, what a grand sight,
He juggles acorns, pure delight.

The trees chuckle, their branches sway,
As birds sing tunes to end the day.
Old boughs sway with laughter loud,
While crickets chirp, a night-time crowd.

But even in this playful scene,
A bear sneezes—oh, what a keen!
The dust clouds swirl, they laugh and flee,
In this nutty place, we all agree.

Songs of Solitude in Leafy Depths

When the wind whispers through tall pines,
The frogs all croak their silly lines.
A turtle hums a sleepy tune,
Underneath the watchful moon.

An owl twirls in an awkward way,
Aiming for a dance today.
But ants critique his clumsy style,
And giggle softly all the while.

While shadows stretch and stars arrive,
A hedgehog rolls—oh my, he thrives!
He bumps a branch, it swings of course,
A squirrel scolds, "You're such a force!"

Yet in this place of funny woes,
The laughter grows as friendship flows.
In leafy depths, where joy's the key,
All creatures thrive in harmony.

Tales of the Timeless Terrain

In valleys wide, where stories start,
A gopher dreams of being smart.
He draws up plans with leafy ink,
But all his friends just stop to blink.

A deer jogs by, tripping on grass,
With such style, but oh, alas!
He tumbles down with quite a flair,
While rabbits cheer, "You've got to share!"

The trees all lean to hear the news,
As a crow caws, wearing bright shoes.
"Look at me!" he proudly brags,
While pigeons join with petty jags.

The tales unfold, twist and bend,
In timeless ways, they never end.
With giggles, roots, and grassy cheers,
This land of jest brings happy years.

Whispered Secrets of the Woodlands

In quiet woods where secrets dwell,
A mouse spins yarns, oh so swell.
His friends all gather, ears on high,
For tales that make the owls sigh.

"Did you see how the badger slipped?
He thought he'd dance but truly tripped!"
With every tale, the laughter grows,
A chorus of giggles softly flows.

Through twinkling lights and rustling leaves,
The forest breathes, and mischief weaves.
A hedgehog claims he found a crown,
But raccoons giggle, "Oh, sit down!"

Yet here amid the whispered fun,
Each secret shared is surely spun.
So come on through, enjoy the tease,
In woodlands filled with silly ease.

Stories Woven in Gnarled Branches

In the woods where squirrels play,
A raccoon once lost his way.
He thought a twig was a fancy pie,
But it just made the other critters sigh.

The branches twist like old man's hair,
They gossip low, without a care.
A wise owl hoots a joke or two,
While a chipmunk laughs, 'What else is new?'

Beneath the moss, a turtle grins,
His shell adorned with bygone wins.
He'll tell you tales of pranks and schemes,
As fireflies dance and share their dreams.

So listen close to forest's cheer,
In gnarled branches, laughter's near.
For every tree has its own fun tale,
In this silly, leafy, winding trail.

The Serenade of Sunlit Glades

In glades where sunlight spills like wine,
A frog once sang, claiming he could shine.
But as he croaked, a bird flew by,
And teased him back, 'Oh me, oh my!'

Butterflies laughed, flitting about,
"Is that a song? Or a funny shout?"
A bumblebee buzzed with glee so bold,
"Your tunes are worth their weight in gold!"

The grass tickled as they all did sway,
To nature's tunes, in a funny play.
So if you wander through this glade,
Expect to find a funny parade!

For every leaf and every sound,
Is a merry tale waiting to be found.
So join the dance, let laughter reign,
In sunlit glades where joy is plain.

Echoes of Nature's Past

In echoing woods where whispers drift,
Old legends spin in a comical lift.
The trees recall of battles fought,
Between raccoons and a cat, who got caught.

A squirrel once thought he found a crown,
But it was just a cap turned upside down!
He wore it proud through the leafy maze,
And all the critters had a giggling phase.

Yet shadows dance with tales to share,
Of forgotten pranks and woodland flair.
So gather round, and hear the cheer,
For nature's echoes always draw near.

In roots and branches, laughter leans,
As stories bloom in all their greens.
So take a stroll, enjoy the fun,
In nature's past, we all are one.

Roots That Recount Forgotten Times

Beneath the ground, the roots do chuckle,
With secrets held in earthy snuggle.
They spoke of trolls who baked big pies,
And creatures with more legs than eyes.

A wise old root paused to declare,
"Remember the jesters who danced on air?"
A gust of wind joined in with zest,
Blowing tales of who danced best.

One root claimed it was truly grand,
To slide down hills of soft, brown sand.
While another whispered with glee and pride,
Of the times they hid when storms collided.

So gather round the old bark tree,
To hear the roots laugh joyously.
For every twist and turn that binds,
Are tales of laughter through forgotten minds.

Sapling Dreams and Elder Wisdom

In the glade where saplings sway,
Old trees chuckle at their play.
Roots like boots in muddy mire,
Laughing loud, they never tire.

Little leaves with daring plans,
Swinging like they're in a band.
Elders whisper, "Stay in line!"
But the little ones just shine.

Tiny sprouts with dreams so grand,
Think they're taller than they stand.
Oaks just grin, they know their fate,
"Patience, kids, just wait—don't hate!"

Branches stretch to touch the sky,
Spinning tales of how they fly.
Elder bark gives sage advice,
"Be a goof, but not too nice!"

Beneath the Watchful Oak

Under branches wide and grand,
Critters gather, join the band.
Squirrels chatter, making plans,
While rabbits hop in silly dance.

"Hey, look here!" a badger said,
"Raccoons tread where angels dread!"
Beneath the oak, they share their jest,
And laughing hearts declare the best.

"Don't eat my acorns!" cries a jay,
As friends roll leaves in gleeful play.
The sun peeks through, a teasing light,
In this woodland, all feels right.

With whispers soft, the oak does nod,
"Join the fun? Just don't be odd!"
And so they laugh and take their chance,
In nature's grand and funny dance.

The Path Hemmed in Green

Along the trail where grasses grow,
Silly blooms put on a show.
"Who's the brightest?" petals sway,
While weeds try hard to join the fray.

"Step right up!" a dandelion yells,
"I'm the king of pollen's smells!"
But thistles puff and strike a pose,
With prickly pride that nobody knows.

Curvy paths with twists and turns,
Every corner, nature churns.
"Keep it cool!" a wise owl hoots,
While frogs make merry with their toots.

Laughter echoes through the glade,
Where silly sunbeams love to fade.
Nature chuckles, feels so spry,
As creatures play, and days float by.

Moonlight on the Wooden Floor

Under stars, the night does gleam,
Wooden floors where shadows dream.
Mice in capes with tiny swords,
Planning heists of leftover cords.

The moon peeks in, a curious guest,
While owls hoot, they jest and jest.
"Stealth is key!" the leader squeaks,
As laughter dances in the weeks.

The sugary crumbs are the goal,
For tiny paws and gleeful souls.
Through the night, they plot and scheme,
In moonlight's glow, they chase their dream.

Yet dawn comes soft with morning glow,
Scurrying off, they're quick to go.
The night was filled with fun and cheer,
As dreams of crumbs start to disappear.

www.ingramcontent.com/pod-product-compliance
Lightning Source LLC
Chambersburg PA
CBHW071846160426
43209CB00003B/432